Construction Machines

Bulldozers

Dash!
LEVELED READERS
An Imprint of Abdo Zoom • abdobooks.com

2

2

Dash!
LEVELED READERS

Level 1 – Beginning
Short and simple sentences with familiar words or patterns for children who are beginning to understand how letters and sounds go together.

Level 2 – Emerging
Longer words and sentences with more complex language patterns for readers who are practicing common words and letter sounds.

Level 3 – Transitional
More developed language and vocabulary for readers who are becoming more independent.

abdobooks.com

Published by Abdo Zoom, a division of ABDO, PO Box 398166, Minneapolis, Minnesota 55439. Copyright © 2019 by Abdo Consulting Group, Inc. International copyrights reserved in all countries. No part of this book may be reproduced in any form without written permission from the publisher. Dash!™ is a trademark and logo of Abdo Zoom.

Printed in the United States of America, North Mankato, Minnesota.
092018
012019

Photo Credits: iStock, Shutterstock
Production Contributors: Kenny Abdo, Jennie Forsberg, Grace Hansen, John Hansen
Design Contributors: Dorothy Toth, Neil Klinepier

Library of Congress Control Number: 2018945598

Publisher's Cataloging in Publication Data

Names: Murray, Julie, author.
Title: Bulldozers / by Julie Murray.
Description: Minneapolis, Minnesota : Abdo Zoom, 2019 | Series: Construction machines | Includes online resources and index.
Identifiers: ISBN 9781532125133 (lib. bdg.) | ISBN 9781641856584 (pbk.) | ISBN 9781532126154 (ebook) | ISBN 9781532126666 (Read-to-me ebook)
Subjects: LCSH: Bulldozers--Juvenile literature. | Construction equipment--Juvenile literature. | Machinery--Construction--Juvenile literature.
Classification: DDC 624.152--dc23

Table of Contents

Bulldozers 4

Different Jobs 12

More Facts 22

Glossary 23

Index 24

Online Resources 24

Bulldozers

Bulldozers are big machines. They are powerful earthmovers!

A bulldozer has many parts. The operator sits in the cab. A large metal blade is on the front. The blade can move up and down.

Bulldozers move on tracks. They have wide ridges. These help them move over bumpy ground.

A bulldozer has a **ripper** on the back. It has sharp claws. It breaks up hard ground.

Different Jobs

Bulldozers are used for many different jobs. They move dirt and rocks.

They are used to help build roads and buildings.

They are also used to clear land. They can push trees over.

Bulldozers are helpful at **landfills**. They move trash around.

They can even be used to help clear snow off of roads!

More Facts

- The first bulldozer design was made in 1923. A replica is on display in Morrowville, Kansas.

- Caterpillar is the largest bulldozer manufacturer in the United States.

- The military uses bulldozers. They have special armor to protect them in combat.

Glossary

landfill – the site used for waste disposal.

ripper – a long claw-like device that helps to loosen tough or solid ground.

Index

landfill 19

operator 6

parts 6, 8, 11

snow 20

terrain 8

tracks 8

uses 4, 13, 14, 16, 19, 20

Online Resources

Booklinks
NONFICTION NETWORK
FREE! ONLINE NONFICTION RESOURCES

To learn more about bulldozers, please visit **abdobooklinks.com**. These links are routinely monitored and updated to provide the most current information available.